The Dinner Party

NEIL SIMON

The Dinner Party

GARDEN CITY, NEW YORK

Manufactured in the U.S.A.

ISBN: 0-7394-2087-9

Neil Simon's THE DINNER PARTY opened October 19, 2000, at The Music Box. It was produced by Emanuel Azenberg, Ira Pittelman, Eric Krebs, Scott Nederlander, ShowOnDemand.com and Center Theatre Group/Mark Taper Forum/Gordon Davidson. It was directed by John Rando. Scenic design was by John Lee Beatty, costume design was by Jane Greenwood, lighting design was by Brian MacDevitt and sound design was by Jon Gottlieb. Technical supervision was provided by Unitech. The production supervisor was David O'Brien. Casting was by Jay Binder CSA and Amy Lieberman. The press representative was Bill Evans & Associates, marketing was provided by the Nancy Richards Group, media advisor was Alan Bernhard and general manager was Abbie M. Strassler. Associate producers were Ginger Montel and Marcia Roberts.

THE CAST

Albert .... Henry Winkler
Claude .... John Ritter
Andre .... Len Cariou
Gabrielle .... Penny Fuller
Yvonne .... Veanne Cox
Mariette .... Jan Maxwell

ACT ONE

THE DINNER PARTY

A private dining room in a first rate restaurant in Paris. The present. At stage right is a dining table, set for six.

Against the wall at stage left is a long serving table with large silver tureens of food with bottles of champagne, a few already open.

In the center of the room is a small sofa for two and a chair on each side of the sofa. Everything in the room, from furniture to the wall decorations are French and softly attractive.

At Rise:
Claude Pichon, early forties, in black tie, stands alone in the room, looks at his watch and sips champagne. He looks a little lost. He looks at the dining table, then crosses to the buffet table, lifts tureen covers, sniffs food, then over to the hors d'oeuvres and samples a few. Turns and looks lost again.

There is a double door almost at rear center stage. Another door, smaller, on the side wall. The large door opens and another man enters, about the same age, in black tie as well. This is Albert Donay.

ALBERT: Hello. Am I in the right place? The Gerard party?

CLAUDE: Yes. Well, I think so. I'm the first one here.

(*Albert comes in, closes the door*)

ALBERT: I'm Albert Donay.

CLAUDE: Claude Pichon.

(*They shake hands. Albert winces in pain, pulls his hand away and tries to shake off pain*)

ALBERT: AHHH . . . Ooooh.

CLAUDE: I'm sorry. Did I do that?

ALBERT: No, I did. Hurt my finger putting my tie on.

CLAUDE: Yes, bow ties are a bother. Did you make it yourself?

ALBERT: No, it's my father's. He snapped it while my finger was up. (*Holds his finger to his throat*) This is *very* nice, isn't it?

CLAUDE: Well, it *is* La Cassette . . . They say that Josephine lived here once . . . Napoleon used to visit her secretly through that door. (*He points to the small door*)

ALBERT: Really? How convenient to have a restaurant in your own home.

CLAUDE: I er, don't think it was a restaurant then.

ALBERT: Of course not. This is all new to me . . . I rarely come into Paris.

CLAUDE: Of course.

ALBERT: Any idea who's coming tonight?

CLAUDE: No, not a clue.

ALBERT: Same here . . . Are you er . . . alone?

CLAUDE: Alone? Yes.

ALBERT: I thought perhaps your wife . . .

CLAUDE: No, no. I'm not married.

ALBERT (*pointing*)**:** Ah . . . but you still wear your wedding band.

CLAUDE: No, It comes off. (*He slides it off*) Depends on whether you want to be available or *un*available. (*He slides it back and forth*) You make your choice when you see who your dinner partner's going to be.

ALBERT: Very practical.

CLAUDE: You go to enough dinner parties, you hear wedding bands sliding on and off all around you . . . You have no ring so I assume you're single.

ALBERT: Yes, I am.

CLAUDE: Never married?

ALBERT: Twice. Both to the same woman.

CLAUDE: Ah. And both marriages failed?

ALBERT: Well, obviously the first marriage was better than the second otherwise there'd be no point going back for another try.

CLAUDE: I can see that. (*Claude sips his champagne as Albert crosses and pours himself a drink*) Any idea what this party's about?

ALBERT: Not a clue. I was hoping you did.

CLAUDE: Except, of course, that Paul's hosting it.

ALBERT: Paul?

CLAUDE: Paul Gerard, the attorney.

ALBERT: Paul, of course. Had it on my calendar for weeks. My secretary reminded me this morning. She gave me the address, the time, didn't write down the name. Just assumed I remembered it was Paul.

CLAUDE: So you're very busy then.

ALBERT: No, my secretary is.

CLAUDE: What is it you do, if I may ask?

ALBERT: I'm in the auto industry.

CLAUDE: Really? In production?

ALBERT: No. Rentals.

CLAUDE: I see . . . You find it interesting?

ALBERT: God, no. Bores me to death. It's my father's business . . . Actually, I'm an artist. Studied at the Academy.

CLAUDE: Good for you. What sort of paintings do you do?

ALBERT: Cars, mostly. In the abstract. Well, they're all out there sitting on the lot posing for me . . . I don't need a studio.

CLAUDE: Abstract cars? Much of a market for that?

ALBERT: Well, people come there to rent cars, not buy paintings . . . I tried renting the paintings once, it didn't work out.

CLAUDE: Do you like Fragonard? (*Claude indicates the mural on back wall*)

ALBERT: Not before dinner, no.

CLAUDE: The artist, Fragonard. That mural is in the style of Fragonard. Around 1786.

ALBERT (*looks at mural*)**:** Actually I paint in the style of Range Rover . . . If the customer wants, I paint in their name on the license plate.

CLAUDE: Clever.

ALBERT: And what do you do?

CLAUDE: I have a shop. Antique books. Classics, mostly. First editions . . . Victor Hugo, Emile Zola, Charles Dickens.

ALBERT: How lucky for you. To spend your days with people like that.

CLAUDE: Well, they don't exactly come into the shop.

ALBERT: Oh, but they do. They're there on your shelves, night and day, just waiting for someone to open their pages . . . Do you ever find personal letters from very famous people?

CLAUDE: Well, I have an Albert Einstein letter to his cousin, a relative in Austria.

ALBERT: Einstein's relative? Do you think that's where he got the idea for his—

CLAUDE: Don't even go there. (*Looks around*) I wonder where the others are. Today is the seventeenth, isn't it?

ALBERT (*holds up his watch, squints at it*)**:** I can't tell. They print the dates so small, you need a microscope. And the face doesn't have any numbers. But it's the in thing they say. (*Shows it to Claude*)

CLAUDE: So what's the advantage of the watch?

ALBERT: It was on sale.

CLAUDE: Right. Lower the prices . . . Maybe that's what you should do with your paintings.

ALBERT: I've tried that. I sold six frames, no paintings . . . Are you always so prompt for things like this?

CLAUDE: I wasn't prompt. I was early . . . *You* were prompt.

ALBERT: Right . . . Large party, you suppose?

CLAUDE: I wouldn't think so. There's only six places for dinner. (*He points to the dining table*)

ALBERT: Does Paul usually give small parties?

CLAUDE: I've never been to *any* of his parties.

ALBERT: Nor have I. I don't party much. I usually paint at night.

CLAUDE: Yes, your car series, of course . . . Do you ever paint *people*?

ALBERT: Only if they're in the cars.

CLAUDE: Of course. It's what you call . . . "your style" . . . So you're really not a close friend of Paul's.

ALBERT: He handled my divorce.

CLAUDE: Really? He handled mine as well . . . Did he do well by you?

ALBERT: It was a difficult time.

CLAUDE: Tell me about it.

ALBERT: Oh, it's a long story . . .

CLAUDE: No, it's just an expression. "Tell me about it," meaning I've had the same problems. You never heard that expression?

ALBERT: Not really. I don't go out to lunch much . . . (*He looks around*) Ever been here before?

CLAUDE: La Cassette? Just once. In the upstairs restaurant. A bit steep for me. The food, of course, is first rate.

ALBERT: I'm not much into rich foods. I have simple tastes . . . No organs . . . No lungs, no kidneys, no liver, et cetera.

CLAUDE: No meat at all?

ALBERT: Some . . . as long as the meat doesn't have any body function.

CLAUDE: I see your point.

ALBERT (*looks around*)**:** No waiters, I notice.

CLAUDE: Yes. I notice that too. Apparently this is to be a very *intimate* dinner.

ALBERT: I agree. It all has a bit of the mystique about it, don't you think?

CLAUDE: In what way?

ALBERT: In a mystique way. Vague. Cryptic. Enigmatic. Ambiguous.

CLAUDE: How do you mean?

ALBERT (*looks at him, puzzled*)**:** Pretty much what I've said. I've used up all my synonyms.

CLAUDE: You mean hard to put your finger on.

ALBERT: Yes. I forgot that one. Hard to put your finger on.

CLAUDE: Perhaps it's *meant* to be. Secretive, I mean.

ALBERT: Secretive, that's another good word. But why?

CLAUDE: It could be a surprise party.

ALBERT: Why would he invite *me* to a surprise party? I don't know any of his friends. Do you?

CLAUDE: Since I don't know who's coming, I don't *know* if I know them.

ALBERT: Perhaps we got on the list by mistake.

CLAUDE: No. He's too good a lawyer to make an error like that.

ALBERT: Well, maybe he's good at legal things but not at party things.

(*The entrance door opens and a man leans in. This is Andre. An attractive man, dressed in a neat gray business suit with a smart shirt and tie*)

ANDRE: Excuse me, is this the Paul Gerard affair?

CLAUDE: We believe so. Just getting under way.

ANDRE: Am I the first to arrive?

ALBERT: No. We are.

(*They are standing close together*)

ANDRE: You're guests? . . . I thought you were waiters.

CLAUDE: Waiters? Drinking champagne? (*Smiles*) I'm afraid not.

ANDRE: Good God, it's black tie. I didn't know.

CLAUDE: Really? It's on the invitation.

ALBERT (*to Claude*)**:** Actually it wasn't. But the card was so festive. All those blue ribbons tied in a bow. I just assumed—

CLAUDE: I assumed, as well.

ANDRE: If it didn't say black tie, then it isn't black tie.

(*Claude and Albert look at each other*)

CLAUDE: Do we have time to go home and change?

ALBERT: I rented the suit. I have to have it back by ten.

CLAUDE: Is that a problem for you?

ALBERT: Well, I rented the shoes, too. The shirt isn't mine. The tie is my father's. My father is not the problem—

CLAUDE: Some other time. (*Crosses to Andre*) I'm Claude Pichon.

ANDRE: Andre Bouville. (*They shake hands*)

ALBERT: Albert Donay. (*They shake, Albert pulls his hand away in pain*)

ANDRE: I'm sorry.

ALBERT: It's all right. It's a small bow tie injury. (*Holds his finger to his neck*)

CLAUDE: Maybe you can shed some light on this, Bouville.

ANDRE: On what?

CLAUDE: The reason for this dinner party.

ANDRE: I didn't know it *was* a dinner party.

CLAUDE: Didn't you receive an invitation?

ANDRE: No, I was away on business. My office sent me a fax. "Be at La Cassette, private dining room, Tuesday the 17th, eight p.m., Paul Gerard."

ALBERT: And you didn't put "dining room" and "dinner" together?

ANDRE: I had eighteen meetings in three days. I couldn't put my *socks* together. I just landed at the airport. My pilot had to wake me.

CLAUDE: You have your own pilot?

ANDRE: Yes. He comes with the plane.

CLAUDE: You have your own plane?

ANDRE: It's very common to lease them these days.

ALBERT: I know about leasing. I'm in rentals myself.

ANDRE: Really? What kind of planes?

ALBERT: . . . Non flying . . . Autos, trailers, RVs.

ANDRE: No. No, no, no. Get into leasing planes . . . Is that champagne?

ALBERT: Champagne, yes. I'll get you a glass. (*He crosses to sideboard*)

CLAUDE (*to Andre*)**:** And what business are you in, if I may ask?

ANDRE: Men's apparel. I have a chain of boutiques around the country.

ALBERT (*turns*)**:** Bouvilles, of course. Is that you? My God. You've got shops everywhere you look.

ANDRE: Not everywhere. Location is an art form today. (*Takes wine*) Thank you.

ALBERT: Your marketing campaigns are wonderful. Not that I'm much into clothes myself.

ANDRE: Well, perhaps if you bought instead of rented. (*He sips wine, looks at glass*) The chill is gone. No waiters around?

CLAUDE: No, I think we're on our own tonight.

ANDRE: No waiters at La Cassette? Impossible.

CLAUDE: We think Paul's up to something out of the ordinary here.

ANDRE: Like what?

ALBERT: Something vague. Ambiguous. Hard to put your finger on.

ANDRE: What does that mean?

CLAUDE: Difficult to say. Unclear. Obscure. Evasive.

ALBERT (*to Claude*)**:** Very good. That's three more we forgot.

ANDRE: I haven't a clue what you're both talking about.

CLAUDE: I have a question for you, Andre. Are you married?

ANDRE: No.

CLAUDE: *Never* married?

ANDRE: Once. A few years ago.

CLAUDE: Would you be surprised if I told you that Albert and I are *both* divorced men?

ANDRE: Not at all.

CLAUDE: Why not?

ANDRE: Because wives read invitations more carefully and they would have *told* you it wasn't black tie.

ALBERT: He's got a point.

CLAUDE: Since Paul Gerard represented Albert and myself in our divorces, can I assume he did yours as well?

ANDRE: It would be folly if you didn't.

CLAUDE (*points to dining table*)**:** As you can see, it's clearly a party for six, yet the first three guests are all divorced men who've never set eyes on each other. Do you find that odd?

ANDRE: Oddly, I don't. I've been to dinner parties where I've hardly known a soul.

ALBERT: He's got a point there, as well.

CLAUDE: Were they all men? Were they all divorced?

ANDRE (*getting annoyed*)**:** I could tell that *some* were men. I could tell that some were *women*. Don't know about divorced.

ALBERT: Did the men arrive first? Were there no waiters?

ANDRE: Waiters, yes. No clue as to who arrived first. Some couples were married. Sorry I didn't take notes on this.

CLAUDE: Ah, but we have no waiters. We have no women. We have no married couples.

ANDRE (*testily*): It's only five past eight, for God's sakes. And women generally take longer to dress than men. Women also prefer making a later entrance than men.

ALBERT (*to Claude*): He's got an excellent point there.

CLAUDE: But we *can* agree that this dinner is only for people that Paul Gerard helped get divorced.

ANDRE: Six people? It would be more like six hundred. And Paul Gerard has more sensitivity than to throw such a sordid party.

ALBERT: Sordid? My divorces weren't sordid. They were painful.

CLAUDE: Mine was sordid but let's push on.

ANDRE: Push on, Pichon. (*He goes to get a drink*)

CLAUDE (*to Andre*): Who then, are the other three guests?

ANDRE: Well, obviously Paul and his wife, who are *not* divorced, which leaves the sixth guest unaccounted for.

CLAUDE: Ah, but what if Paul is not *bringing* his wife? What, if in fact, Paul and his wife were *themselves* divorcing?

ANDRE: Highly unlikely.

CLAUDE: Why?

ANDRE: They celebrated their thirty-second anniversary yesterday.

CLAUDE: Have you heard from them *today*? Maybe things didn't go well last night.

ANDRE: What's the word I'm looking for?

CLAUDE: Logical?

ANDRE: Inane. Completely inane.

ALBERT: Why don't we wait and see who shows up?

CLAUDE: Fine. In the meantime, let's examine Paul Gerard. What kind of man is he?

ANDRE (*to Claude*)**:** Do you do this for a living? A private detective who works dinner parties?

ALBERT: No. He's an antique book dealer.

ANDRE (*to Albert*)**:** I wasn't serious, Albert. If you thought I was serious, I can't help you.

CLAUDE: Tell me, Andre, what would you say was Paul Gerard's most interesting quality?

ANDRE: That he doesn't screen his clients too well.

ALBERT: There's no need for that, Andre.

ANDRE: I thought there was. I thought there was a very *great* need for that.

ALBERT (*to Andre*)**:** What I meant was that Claude spends his life among the greatest literary minds in the world, and I believe you owe him an apology.

ANDRE: I simply meant that Claude's constant questions were extremely irritating. But you're right, Albert. I must never judge a book by the man who dusts its cover.

ALBERT: That is outrageous. (*He turns away*)

CLAUDE: Shall I tell you what *I* think Paul's most interesting quality is?

ANDRE (*to Claude*)**:** Is there *nothing* that interferes with your continuity?

CLAUDE: I think Paul's most interesting quality is his sensitivity.

ANDRE: I said that before. (*To Albert*) Do you have a cigarette?

ALBERT: I don't smoke.

ANDRE: Well, you should.

CLAUDE: And as a sensitive man, Paul did everything he could to talk me out of this divorce.

ANDRE (*to Albert*)**:** Does he always go on like this?

ALBERT: I've only known him a few minutes.

CLAUDE: "Are you sure you want this?" Paul said to me. "Have you really tried to make this marriage work?"

ANDRE: Do you think he hears what we're saying?

CLAUDE: And I thought to myself, "How sensitive of Paul. A lawyer willing to deprive himself of a very large fee."

ANDRE (*to Albert*)**:** Do you think he assumes we left the room?

CLAUDE: No, I see you there . . . Now, knowing what we know so far, who do you think is going to be the next one to walk through that door?

ANDRE: The tailor coming to collect Albert's rented suit . . . *Why do you insist on pursuing this?* It's idiotic.

CLAUDE (*smiles*)**:** You know, I find you delightful, Andre. You have a witty, caustic sense of humor and you hold nothing back. And, strangely, I'm not offended by it.

ANDRE: Then I must be doing it wrong.

ALBERT: See, I find *that* offensive.

ANDRE: Thank you, Albert. At least *you* understand me.

CLAUDE: Would either of you like to hear who *I* think will come through that door?

ANDRE: As if we'd get out of here alive if we didn't.

CLAUDE: I say it's a woman. Attractive. Age, between thirty and thirty-eight. And unattached.

ALBERT: How would you know she's unattached?

ANDRE (*to Albert*)**:** There's three single men here. A gentleman like Paul would never send in a married woman.

CLAUDE: Very good, Andre.

ANDRE: I hate when he agrees with me.

ALBERT (*to Andre*)**:** I wish you would stop doing that.

ANDRE (*to Albert*)**:** I wish you were a cigarette.

CLAUDE: Now then, who would the *following* two guests be?

ALBERT: Well, now it's obvious. Two more women . . . Am I right?

CLAUDE: You are right, Albert . . . Two attractive women *and*—available.

ALBERT: Available for what?

CLAUDE (*smirks*)**:** Well, I would say that very much depends on us.

ANDRE: It's your opinion that Paul Gerard, one of the most respected men in his profession, is going to pimp for us.

CLAUDE: I said nothing of the kind. In fact, I would think that these were respectable women. It's my guess that Paul feels guilty for not being able to save our marriages and now he's making up for it. He's looking out for us.

ANDRE: So he's sending three respectable women to soothe our aching hearts. Therefore, he's *not* a pimp. He's a *pimporetto*.

ALBERT: If that's true, that's very decent of him.

ANDRE: If it's true, and I'm sure it's not, I don't *need* to meet someone new. I've already *met* someone new. So in that regard, this party is a complete waste of time for me. Goodbye. (*He heads for the door*)

CLAUDE: You can't leave. It would be a great insult to Paul.

ANDRE: I'm just going to get cigarettes . . . Please talk about me while I'm gone. (*He leaves, closes door*)

CLAUDE: What a *huge* pompous ass!

(*Door opens, Andre looks in*)

ANDRE: But with the right suit, no one notices it. (*He smiles, leaves, closes door*)

ALBERT (*to Claude*)**:** He got you on that one, too.

CLAUDE: He's a snob who's above all this. He won't stay long. That means three women for just the two of us. I like our chances. (*He starts for the door on other side of room*)

ALBERT: Where are you going?

CLAUDE: Unfortunately, to the men's room. If a woman arrives, make no advances until I return. Understood?

ALBERT: I understand, but it's not binding.

CLAUDE: I'm sorry but I was the first one here.

ALBERT: And now you're the first one going to the men's room.

CLAUDE: Don't underestimate me, Albert. I'm more experienced with these things than you.

ALBERT: If you were, you would have gone to the men's room before you got here.

CLAUDE (*opens the single door on the side*)**:** I didn't have to then. But I get my pick of the next two.

ALBERT: Not acceptable.

CLAUDE: Why not?

ALBERT: I might not like the first one and you could still be in the men's room.

CLAUDE: I'll see that I'm not. I think you've picked up some bad habits from your friend, Bouville. (*He goes out angrily, closes door*)

ALBERT: *My* friend?? He disliked *me* even *more* than he disliked you . . . *My* friend?

(*Albert looks over the hors d'oeuvres and pops one in his mouth. He likes it and pops another in his mouth*)

(*The entrance door opens. A woman comes in. This is Mariette. About 36 or 37. Attractive in a smart suit. Albert does not see her yet.*)

MARIETTE: Excuse me. Is this the Gerard party?

(*Albert embarrassed, turns, nods, trying to swallow the hors d'oeuvre. He holds up his finger for her to wait*)

ALBERT: Hmm?

MARIETTE: The Gerard dinner party?

(*Albert holds up his finger again, turns his back to her for a moment, tries hard to swallow fast. Wipes his mouth with a napkin quickly, then turns*)

ALBERT (*with food in his mouth*)**:** I'm thorry, I haven't . . . (*He swallows*) I'm sorry. I haven't eaten all day. (*He wipes his mouth, then turns back to her*) The Gerard dinner party? Yes. It is.

MARIETTE (*looks around*)**:** Are we the first?

ALBERT: No. I'm the second, you're the fourth. Please come in. (*She does. He closes the door behind her*) I'm Albert Donay.

MARIETTE: How do you do? Mariette Levieux.

(*They shake. Albert bites his lip, trying to quiet the pain. We hear a little painful murmur as he tries to smile.*)

MARIETTE: Are you all right?

ALBERT: Oh, yes. I do that when I'm happy to meet someone. (*She looks at him queerly*) . . . Is it Miss Levieux?

MARIETTE: Yes . . . Where's one and three?

ALBERT: Pardon?

MARIETTE: If we're two and four . . . ?

ALBERT: Ah. Yes. One and three. Three went to get cigarettes and one went to the men's room.

MARIETTE: Yes.

ALBERT: Would you care for a glass of champagne?

MARIETTE: That would be very nice, thank you.

ALBERT (*goes to get drink*)**:** It's very odd but number one just said that he was quite sure that number four would be a woman.

MARIETTE: Did he? Why is that odd?

ALBERT (*pours champagne*)**:** Because one, two, and three are all men. (*He crosses with champagne*)

MARIETTE: Are they? . . . Is there some reason why we're all referred to as numbers?

ALBERT: No, no. Except it might confuse you if I said names of people you hadn't met yet. (*He gives her champagne*)

MARIETTE: Well, I know you're Albert and you know I'm Mariette so I think that's a good start.

ALBERT (*smiles*)**:** An excellent start.

MARIETTE: This is a lovely room. (*Looks at dining table*) Are we just six for dinner?

ALBERT: It would appear that way . . . It's Albert, remember?

MARIETTE: Yes. You told me.

ALBERT: I know. I meant in case you wanted to use it.

MARIETTE: Thank you, Albert, I will . . . I suppose five and six are Paul Gerard and his wife?

ALBERT: We don't really know that. There's even some conjecture that the Gerards won't be coming.

MARIETTE: To their own party? Why would they do that?

ALBERT: There was some confusion about that also. By one and three. And by two, I *was* two, but now I'm Albert . . . Did the Gerards give you any hint?

MARIETTE: Actually, I never spoke to them.

ALBERT: But you are a friend of the Gerards?

MARIETTE: Not to Paul. Just his wife. But he wrote me such a charming letter enclosed in the invitation, I decided to accept.

ALBERT (*smiles*)**:** I'm glad you did . . . By the way, it's not black tie. I misread the invitation.

MARIETTE: Are you saying I'm overdressed?

ALBERT: No. You look absolutely perfect. Actually, *I'm* overdressed. And number one, too . . . I mean number one *is* too . . . Number three *may* have gotten it right. I have no idea what five and six are wearing.

MARIETTE: Since you don't know who they are.

ALBERT: Exactly.

MARIETTE: And if it's not the Gerards, who might it be?

ALBERT: Well, Claude . . . he's number one . . . Claude thought that perhaps the Gerards selected three women to come to dinner.

MARIETTE: Which women?

ALBERT: Most likely three women who don't know each other.

MARIETTE: You mean six total strangers?

ALBERT: Not total. We all seem to have some connection to Paul Gerard. Am I making myself clear?

MARIETTE: Perhaps, but not to me . . . For three men who don't know each other, you seem to have gotten very involved.

ALBERT: Well, one and two were more involved than I was.

MARIETTE: I thought you were two.

ALBERT: Involved? No, not as much.

MARIETTE: That you were *number* two.

ALBERT: Ah, right. (*He spills his drink*) Sorry.

(Pulls out handkerchief and spreads it on floor. He helps her across. As she crosses, Albert wipes the spill up with his handkerchief. He crosses to her holding the handkerchief in one hand, the champagne flute in the other) If you didn't know who was coming or what you were coming to, why did you come?

MARIETTE: Very simple. I thought it was time for me to get out and meet new people.

ALBERT: That's why *I* came. *(He looks for a place to put the wet handkerchief. Seeing none he squeezes the champagne from the handkerchief into the flute, followed by the handkerchief itself)* And that's what you and I are doing now. *(Looks for a place to put the flute. Not finding one he puts it in his inside jacket pocket)* Aren't we?

MARIETTE: No, I meant that I was interested in meeting new *people* as opposed to just one person. I don't think I'm ready for just one person, yet. Please don't take that personally.

ALBERT *(he crosses and places the flute on small table)***:** No. I understand. What you mean is, you want to meet a diversified group of people instead of one specific person.

MARIETTE: Yes.

ALBERT: But what if in that diversified group of people you met one particular person who was more unique than anyone in that combined diversified group? Would you be against that?

MARIETTE: I don't know. This is the first time in my life having a conversation like this.

ALBERT: It's my first time too. (*Mariette starts to leave, Albert backs up to doors blocking her way*) If I seem forward, I assure you I'm not. I'm quite a reserved person, but you seem so easy to talk to.

MARIETTE: Well, that may have something to do with the number of people talking, don't you think? (*She looks around*) If you'll excuse me a moment, I have a rather urgent phone call to make. (*Albert opens the door for her*)

ALBERT: I'll be waiting right here.

MARIETTE (*halfway out the door*)**:** I'm sure you will.

ALBERT: Albert.

MARIETTE (*from hallway*)**:** Albert.

(*She leaves. Albert closes the door behind her. At that moment, Claude comes back through the side door*)

CLAUDE: I have one other theory, Albert. Listen to this . . .

ALBERT: You missed her. Number four. You were right. She was a woman.

CLAUDE: Damn! What did she look like?

ALBERT: Just as you described. *Very* attractive. Maybe late thirties. Very bright. Not the kind who would like Andre at all . . . And very available.

CLAUDE: How do you know?

ALBERT: She said it was time to get out and meet new people.

CLAUDE: What did I tell you? Where is she?

ALBERT: Had to make a phone call. Said it was urgent. By the way, we hit it off *extremely* well.

CLAUDE: Which is not to say she and I won't.

ALBERT: No, no. You forfeited that when you went to the men's room.

CLAUDE: I forfeited nothing if she prefers me.

ALBERT: We agreed that if I preferred her, you would get five and six.

CLAUDE: If I found five and six to my liking . . . Don't forget, I have seniority here.

ALBERT: How do you know you're older than I am?

CLAUDE: Not *older*. Earlier. I was here first.

ALBERT: And I was here *promptly*. Promptly has precedence over coming too early.

CLAUDE: And wasn't it I who said "It's a woman. Attractive. Age between thirty and thirty-eight and unattached?"

ALBERT: Well, now you're too *late*. She attached herself to me.

CLAUDE: And she could *promptly un*attach herself just as fast.

(*The door opens and a smoking Andre enters*)

ANDRE: The Gerards are not coming. Housekeeper said they're in Sardinia.

CLAUDE: Exactly what I predicted.

ANDRE: You never once mentioned Sardinia.

ALBERT (*to Andre*)**:** You just missed number four. She was here.

ANDRE: In the black evening suit. Yes, I saw her coming out.

ALBERT: Very attractive, I thought.

ANDRE: I always thought she was.

CLAUDE: Do you know her?

ANDRE: We dated after my divorce. And hers. We went to Morocco for a weekend.

ALBERT: Really? She doesn't seem the type to do that.

ANDRE: Go to Morocco?

ALBERT: With you.

ANDRE: Albert, you're actually being rude.

ALBERT: Claude says I'm picking it up from you.

CLAUDE (*to Andre*)**:** How did it go in Morocco?

ANDRE: Amusing. But then I met someone else. As did she.

ALBERT: You have no right making her personal business public.

ANDRE: I'm not making it public. I'm just telling you and Claude in private.

CLAUDE: Did she see you just now?

ANDRE: No, she was going in the opposite direction. As I'm about to do myself. Since we now know what this dinner is about, and since I've already *dated* what this dinner's about, I leave the rest for you. (*He heads for the door*)

CLAUDE: You can't walk out. That would be an insult to some innocent, well meaning women.

ANDRE: I can't speak for the others, and Mariette may be well meaning, but I wouldn't exactly say she's an innocent.

CLAUDE: Mariette? Her name's Mariette?

ANDRE: Yes.

CLAUDE: Blonde? About this tall?

ANDRE: That's her.

CLAUDE: Mariette Levieux?

ANDRE: You've dated her?

CLAUDE: On and off. Then on. Then I married her. Then I divorced her . . . He's invited both of us? Christ, why would Paul do that?

ANDRE: To brighten up the party. In lieu of noise-makers and paper hats.

(*The door opens, Mariette enters, looks straight at Claude, angrily*)

MARIETTE: I called your house. They said you were at La Cassette . . . Christ, why would Paul do that?

ANDRE: In lieu of noisemakers and paper hats.

MARIETTE (*turns, looks at Andre*)**:** Oh, Jesus! You're here as well? Christ. Who else is coming? My doctor, dentist, and accountant?

ANDRE: Don't think so. That would make seven.

MARIETTE: If this is a joke, I find it appalling. (*To Claude*) Did you know about this?

CLAUDE: If I did, you think I'd come in black tie to see you wearing the jewelry I paid for?

MARIETTE: This is the nightmare of my life.

CLAUDE: Tonight's may be worse. (*To Albert*) Back to the original plan. I get five and six. (*Claude crosses to bar, picks up scotch and swigs from bottle*)

MARIETTE: I'm leaving before this turns into farce.

ANDRE: It's *already* farce. I think we're aiming for a much higher form of absurdity here.

MARIETTE: I'm going to call Paul Gerard and ask for an explanation.

ANDRE: Sorry. He's in Sardinia.

MARIETTE (*angrily to Albert*)**:** Why didn't you tell me that?

ALBERT (*points to Andre*)**:** Because I didn't go to the phone with him.

CLAUDE (*to Mariette*)**:** I didn't have a *clue* you'd be here.

MARIETTE: You didn't have a clue during our marriage.

ALBERT: Listen, if you two would rather be alone . . .

MARIETTE: Stay here, Albert. You're the only gentleman in the room.

CLAUDE: Gentleman? He was just trading women in here like used cars.

ALBERT (*to Mariette*)**:** I try to be a gentleman, Mariette.

ANDRE (*to Albert*)**:** Well, it's a long, steep climb.

CLAUDE (*to Mariette*)**:** I can't believe you went to Morocco with him.

MARIETTE (*to Andre*)**:** You went *public* with that?

ANDRE: It wasn't a stock offering . . . And I didn't know he was your ex-husband.

MARIETTE: What are my chances of my being in a room alone with three men, two of whom I dislike intensely?

(Restraining herself from hitting Andre and Claude, Mariette crosses away with shawl and purse in hand.

As she passes Albert, she flings her shawl, hitting him in the face. She puts her shawl and purse on sofa and crosses to bar)

CLAUDE (*to Andre*)**:** Did Paul know you knew my ex-wife well enough to take her to Morocco?

ANDRE: There was no reason to tell Paul since there was no reason for me to know you *or* who your ex-wife was.

ALBERT (*to Claude*)**:** Doesn't it bother you hearing this?

CLAUDE: No. It bothers me that I gave her half my *money* to hear this.

ALBERT: It would bother me.

CLAUDE: Why? You're hearing it for free.

MARIETTE (*to Claude*)**:** And I didn't take half your money. You got half of your *own* money.

ALBERT (*to Mariette*)**:** If you knew Paul Gerard was your husband's lawyer, why did you come to this dinner?

MARIETTE: Because Helena and I are best friends.

ALBERT: Who's Helena?

MARIETTE: Paul's wife. Didn't you know?

ALBERT: No. So are you saying that you were the best friend of the woman who was married to the man who represented your husband in divorce?

ANDRE: In the history of speech, that sentence has never been uttered before.

MARIETTE: I don't think Helena knew who Paul was inviting. She knew only that I was looking to meet new people.

CLAUDE: Or maybe she didn't think you'd recognize me now that I'm living on half my own money.

MARIETTE (*to Albert*)**:** Albert, from now on, I don't want that man to address me in the first person.

ALBERT: Do you want me to tell him—because I think he heard you say it.

CLAUDE (*to Mariette*)**:** You came here to meet new people? Didn't you meet enough new people in Morocco?

MARIETTE: I don't consider someone trying to sell me a ride on a camel as new people. Tell him.

ALBERT (*to Claude*)**:** Mariette doesn't consider that someone trying to—

CLAUDE (*to Albert*)**:** Stay out of this. Go outside and paint some used cars.

MARIETTE (*to Albert*)**:** And to put matters straight, I've been completely alone since my break-up with George Ormande.

ALBERT (*to Mariette*)**:** I think this would go better without me in the middle.

CLAUDE (*to Albert*)**:** Who the hell is George Ormande?

ALBERT: I don't know. I'm sure it's not the camel driver.

MARIETTE (*finally to Claude*)**:** He was my attorney in the divorce. You never paid attention to *anything* concerning me, did you?

CLAUDE: Really? (*To Albert*) They why did I pay her all that alimony?

ALBERT: I don't know. I wasn't in the courtroom. (*He walks away*)

ANDRE: As scarcely entertaining as this is, why don't you all calm down while I call Paul in Sardinia and find out exactly what they have planned. (*He turns, looks at Albert*) Albert . . . you have a smudge on your face.

ALBERT: I do? (*He rubs his face and looks at his hand*) Where?

ANDRE: In the men's room.

ALBERT: In the men's room?

ANDRE: Go and look. (*Andre leaves*)

ALBERT (*suddenly gets it*)**:** Oh. Yes, of course. (*To Claude*) I don't think that she—

CLAUDE: I don't want to hear it.

ALBERT (*to Mariette*)**:** Excuse me. I have a smudge—

MARIETTE: Would you please?

(*Albert leaves. Claude and Mariette are alone*)

CLAUDE (*to Mariette*)**:** Well, aren't *you* popular. . . The only woman at the party and already you've met your ex-husband, your ex-lover, *and* your next boyfriend . . . Enjoying yourself Mariette?

MARIETTE: Sorry, but Andre never got to *be* an ex-lover and Albert will *never* be my next boy friend . . . But I'm delighted to have you as an ex-hubby . . . As for me, I intend to be an ex-guest. (*Grabbing her shawl and purse, Mariette heads for door*) I hope you and your friends have an *exquisite* dinner. (*She opens the door*) Excuse me, won't you. (*She goes closing the door behind her*)

CLAUDE (*angrily*)**:** *Ex*traordinary.

(*The side door opens and Albert comes out quickly*)

ALBERT: I heard you two shouting. Mariette seemed very upset.

CLAUDE: She asked you to leave and you listened at the door?

ALBERT: Well, I had nothing else to listen to . . . Is she coming back?

CLAUDE: Did you hear her say *no*? . . . *Why are you always a beat behind?*

ALBERT (*points to watch*)**:** I told you. I can't see the numbers on my watch.

(*The door opens quickly and Mariette comes in*)

MARIETTE: No. I've changed my mind. I'm staying.

ALBERT (*smiles*)**:** I'm so glad you did. I *knew* we—

MARIETTE: Would you please leave us alone, Albert?

ALBERT: Of course. I have a smudge on my face. (*He goes back through small door*)

MARIETTE (*paces before she talks, then*)**:** Claude . . . I know this is awkward, but do you know what I never said to you at our divorce?

CLAUDE: That you'll take less money.

MARIETTE: God! Is that all you divorced men talk about?

CLAUDE: You think there's a club we all go to on Thursday nights and say, "Remember when we had more furniture in this club?"

MARIETTE: If there's anything in my apartment that you really want, come over and get it.

CLAUDE: Fine. What time do you open?

MARIETTE: You were never this materialistic while we were married.

CLAUDE: Of course not. I still had my material.

MARIETTE: Then come take it all. I mean it. Except the jewelry you gave me . . . They mean something to me.

CLAUDE: No. I gave you the jewelry, it's yours . . . By the way, how's my half of the dog?

MARIETTE: Babette is fine, thank you.

CLAUDE: Good. Does she ever bark for me? . . . Or is that not the half I got?

MARIETTE: You can have her any weekend you want . . . Look . . . What I never had a chance to say to you at our divorce, was thank you for sharing your knowledge of literature with me . . . It helped me to become a better writer.

CLAUDE: Thank you . . . I must say, you've had a tremendous success, Mariette.

MARIETTE: Not that you approved of my writing. You thought it was trash, didn't you?

CLAUDE: You mustn't hold me accountable for when I talk in my sleep.

MARIETTE: No. I understand. I know how much you wanted that success for yourself.

CLAUDE: I had my chance . . . It just wasn't in the cards.

MARIETTE: I'm sorry.

CLAUDE: Maybe if you hadn't taken the cards *with* you . . .

MARIETTE: You're impossible. I'm leaving. (*She turns to go*)

CLAUDE: No. *I'll* go. (*He crosses, opens door*)

MARIETTE (*points to his hand*)**:** Why are you still wearing your wedding ring?

CLAUDE: It was the only safe place I knew to keep *you* from getting it. (*He goes, closing the door*)

(*Albert rushes in*)

ALBERT: I heard the door slam. I'm glad you're still here. Where's Claude?

MARIETTE: I've always wondered myself.

(*The large door opens. Andre steps in*)

ANDRE: Paul's line is busy. I heard the door. Has anyone else arrived?

MARIETTE: Yes. I went through that door and came back. Claude went out *that* door but *didn't* come back. Albert came in that door. He's been here until *you* came in the door to tell us Paul's line is busy.

ANDRE: *Very* good. Would you consider working for me?

MARIETTE: Andre, you know I write novels.

ANDRE: Yes, I read one. The offer still stands. (*He leaves*)

ALBERT: This room is so busy. Do you know that Napoleon came in through that door?

MARIETTE: Really? I must have missed him.

CLAUDE (*comes back in*)**:** One last thing . . .

ALBERT: Claude, I think Mariette is very upset now.

MARIETTE: Albert, would you leave us alone, please?

ALBERT: Of course. (*Heads for men's room*) It's just that I don't know what to *do* in there anymore. (*He goes*)

CLAUDE: Do you know why my career didn't flourish, Mariette? Because the writers I aspire to be were beyond my reach. All those in my shop, Voltaire, Victor Hugo, Emile Zola, Thomas Mann . . .

MARIETTE: No. You were right to learn from the best.

CLAUDE: They defeated me. You don't learn to think like Tolstoy. You have to be *born* Tolstoy . . . You don't learn to write like Kafka. You have to have nightmares like Kafka . . . I read passages to you from every book I ever loved because God knows, you would never tackle it on your own.

MARIETTE: Are you begrudging the help you gave me?

CLAUDE: No. I was jealous of what you did with it. Nabokov was too oblique for you so I broke it down and simplified it. Nabokov is great but I'm easier to understand.

MARIETTE: But you *did* teach me. Isn't that satisfying enough?

CLAUDE: Don't you understand? I couldn't translate

even a speck of their genius into my own work. But somehow what I *did* learn went directly to you. It's like secondhand smoke without the nicotine.

MARIETTE: But first rate advice. You were always smarter than me.

CLAUDE: But what I wrote was inferior versions of the classics. What you wrote was superior versions of my inadequate prose which you turned into mediocre fiction, which is exactly what the public wants.

MARIETTE: Why should I write what the public *doesn't* want? And I'm glad the public does because I can't write any better than I do . . . when you read pieces to me from Voltaire and Camus and Proust and Sartre, I absorbed it without even knowing I was listening. Who today can write like they did? But in my own small way, I learned how to write a story, compose a sentence, how to keep a reader's interest before they fall asleep . . . You taught it all to me, Claude. By osmosis. I think your anger comes from thinking I stole from you . . . If I stole anything, it was your passion for the written word. Maybe it's the only thing in the world we still share.

CLAUDE: Aside from the dog.

MARIETTE: I think it was right that we divorced, Claude . . . I just think we did it a little too soon.

(*As he steps toward her, we hear a knock on the door*)

CLAUDE (*screams*)**:** Stay out of here, Albert. We're having a post marital spat.

MARIETTE (*points to big door*)**:** It was *that* door . . . Come in!

(*The big door opens. A pretty young woman, although not too stylishly dressed, comes in. This is Yvonne*)

YVONNE: Oh. Hello. I'm Yvonne Fouchet. I know I'm late for dinner and I apologize but as I was coming here in the taxi, I thought it over and realized it would be a big mistake for me to be here tonight, for reasons of my own. So if you would please give my regards to the Gerards, I'll just call another taxi and leave. It was very nice meeting you both. (*Smiles*) Goodbye. (*She leaves, closing the door*)

CLAUDE (*to Mariette*)**:** Where are these people coming from?

(*The small door opens and Albert rushes in*)

ALBERT: I heard the door again. Did anyone else show up?

MARIETTE: Number five was here but thought it over in the taxi and decided to go home.

ALBERT: Go home? Did she say why?

MARIETTE: Hard to say. She spoke without commas or periods.

ALBERT (*to Claude*)**:** Did you say anything to her?

CLAUDE: No. She did a short comic monologue and left.

ALBERT: What did she look like?

MARIETTE: Like someone I think you would have liked, Albert.

ALBERT: I think I've already *met* someone I like. (*Holding up a silver tray for Mariette to see her face*) Unless you think I'm out of line here, Claude.

CLAUDE: No, I got off that line two years ago. But you can take Mariette home in one of your abstract cars.

MARIETTE: I'm not yours to pass to strangers, Claude.

CLAUDE: He's not a stranger. He's a guest in a rented suit.

ALBERT (*to Mariette*)**:** I'm thinking of buying it.

(*The door opens, Andre comes in*)

ANDRE: Well, it's all settled.

CLAUDE: Did you get through to him?

ANDRE: Oh, yes.

MARIETTE: Did you speak to him?

ANDRE: Oh, yes.

ALBERT: Did he tell you why he gave this party?

ANDRE: Oh, yes. He didn't *give* this party. He just loaned his name. Someone *else* is giving the party.

ALBERT: Did he say who?

ANDRE: Oh, no. What he *did* say was, "Please see it through. All six of you."

CLAUDE: We don't *have* six. Number six hasn't arrived yet and number five *did* arrive but she left.

ANDRE: Why did she leave?

MARIETTE: Because she's smarter than us.

ANDRE (*to Albert*)**:** Why did you let her go?

ALBERT: I never saw her come in.

ANDRE (*crossing to door*)**:** Well, in that case, if she's not coming back, there's definitely no reason for me to stay. (*Andre opens door revealing Yvonne*) Hello. We were expecting you.

YVONNE: I thought it over in the taxi again and decided I would stay after all.

MARIETTE: We were hoping you would. Mariette Levieux?

YVONNE: No. It's Yvonne Fouchet.

MARIETTE: Fine.

CLAUDE: Claude Pichon. (*He crosses and shakes her hand*)

ANDRE: Andre Bouville. (*He crosses and shakes her hand*)

CLAUDE (*points to Albert*)**:** And er . . . he's Albert Donay.

(*Albert nods slightly and turns away*)

YVONNE: Very nice to meet you all . . . Am I the only one here who doesn't know anyone?

MARIETTE: Some of us do. Some of us don't. And some of us don't care.

CLAUDE (*to Yvonne*)**:** Let me get you a chair?

YVONNE: Thank you.

(*Claude stands behind a chair but she sits on empty sofa*)

YVONNE: This may sound stupid but why are we all here?

ANDRE: We're not sure.

YVONNE: Has anyone thought to ask?

CLAUDE (*points to Andre*)**:** He called Sardinia but no luck.

YVONNE: Am I supposed to understand that?

MARIETTE: I think that's what the party's about. To find out what the party's about.

ANDRE (*to Yvonne*)**:** If it's not too personal, may I ask why you left, then decided to come back?

YVONNE: Well, as I was leaving, I saw someone I knew coming up the back stairway. I don't think he saw me. We hadn't seen each other in some time. Well, we did, but we hadn't *spoken* to each other. Well, I did, but he didn't . . . I knew he wouldn't be keen on seeing me so I just got into the taxi and left. And then I said to myself, "No. Although I know he holds a very deep grudge against me, I think it's foolish for two people who were once very close, to ignore each other forever." So I put on my bravest face and came back here to the restaurant.

MARIETTE: Good for you, Yvonne.

CLAUDE (*smirks*)**:** Why would anyone hold a grudge against *you*?

YVONNE: Well, he has good reason. We haven't spoken to each other since our divorce.

ALBERT (*to Mariette*)**:** Not true. I said hello to her at a friend's wedding about a year ago.

YVONNE (*to others*)**:** He didn't say hello. He sort of grunted towards me. But a grunt isn't actual speech.

(*Claude, Mariette, and Andre all look at each other*)

CLAUDE: Puzzle solved. The six guests are all divorced couples. (*Leans over, gloatingly, to Andre*) Looking forward to *that*, Andre?

ANDRE: Sorry to disappoint you, but my ex-wife is dead.

YVONNE: Oh, I'm sorry. You must miss her terribly.

ANDRE (*not concerned*)**:** Well, we were divorced first.

YVONNE: Yes, but she's still dead.

ANDRE: Yes. That's how it works.

YVONNE: Excuse me, but isn't that a rather cold thing to say?

CLAUDE (*to Yvonne*)**:** It gets worse as it goes along.

ANDRE: Is anyone hungry besides me?

CLAUDE (*to Yvonne*)**:** See? He's off the dead wife thing already.

MARIETTE (*to Andre*)**:** If your ex-wife is deceased, and six of us have been invited, who else would you be expecting?

ANDRE: Why should I be expecting *anyone*?

CLAUDE: Because everyone here is a matched set. Is there anyone else in your past life?

ANDRE: My mother. She's eighty-one and lives in Switzerland. So unless she can maneuver her wheelchair down the Alps, I wouldn't count on her. Whoever is behind this, is intent on having a confrontation of couples.

YVONNE: For what purpose?

ANDRE: For the purpose of reviving a dead marriage.

ALBERT (*to Andre*)**:** Well, no one could revive yours unless someone could revive your dead wife. (*They all look at him*) I said that without thinking. Sorry.

YVONNE: Well, in my case it would be a waste of time. Albert and I have no wish to be united. Did you hear we were married and divorced twice?

CLAUDE: Six times.

YVONNE: No, it was twice.

CLAUDE: Yes. We heard *twice* six times.

MARIETTE (*to Yvonne*)**:** You said you came back because you saw Albert on the stairs. But if you weren't talking to him, why come back at all?

YVONNE: It was Albert who wasn't talking to *me*. I came back hoping he would.

ANDRE: In order to win him back?

YVONNE: Not at all. But it's painful to be ignored for the rest of my life. It's an awful feeling to know there's someone out there who hates you that much.

ALBERT (*angrily*)**:** I find it *intolerable* that you're asking her questions about our marriage.

CLAUDE: Well, if *you* won't, what do you care if *we* do?

MARIETTE: I understand your anger, Albert, but in a way I sympathize with Yvonne's situation, as well.

ALBERT: *Her* situation? Do you know anything about *my* situation? What a disappointment you are, Mariette.

MARIETTE: You met me eight minutes ago. That's not enough time to be disappointed.

CLAUDE (*to Mariette*)**:** I met you *nine* years ago. That's plenty enough time for me . . . I'll be at the bar. Andre, care to join me?

ANDRE: No, but I'll go anyway. (*They go, closing the door behind them*)

ALBERT: Then I'm leaving, as well. (*He starts for the door*)

YVONNE: *Please, Mariette. Ask him to stay.*

ALBERT: I'll wait out in the hallway.

YVONNE: *No!* I want him to stay *here*. In this room.

MARIETTE: Albert, she wants you to stay *here*. In this room.

ALBERT: Why? I have no intention of saying a single word to that woman.

YVONNE: Even if he won't speak to me, I have things to say to him.

MARIETTE (*to Albert*)**:** Yvonne is quite willing to do the talking, Albert.

ALBERT: But if I choose not to listen, I won't.

YVONNE: I'll take that chance.

MARIETTE: How conciliatory you are, Yvonne. (*To Albert*) How accessible you are, Albert. (*She starts for the door*) I'll leave you two to have a nice, quiet talk . . . or half a talk, however it goes.

(Mariette smiles at Albert, leaves, and closes the door. Albert and Yvonne are alone. He still hasn't turned to face her.)

YVONNE: . . . So, you're looking well, Albert . . . At least your *back* is looking well . . . Except your shoulders are sagging. That's always a sign that you're unhappy. (*She moves to the chair closer to him*) When I first left, you swore that you would never speak to me as long as you lived. I thought it was just a figure of speech. But you haven't spoken in a year so I guess it's a figure of dead silence. (*He turns, walks to other side of the room, his back still towards her*) I know it hurts when someone leaves and breaks up a marriage. (*Albert holds up two fingers*) *Two* marriages . . . but I never meant to leave you twice. I was satisfied with leaving you just once . . . But you insisted we try it again and we did and it didn't work again . . . So why am I being punished for being right? (*With his back to her, he shakes his head*) I know what shaking your head means. It means that "I just don't get it. That I *never* got it" . . . Well, if you've never said it in words, Albert, what is there to *get*? When you've never given what you claim I haven't gotten? . . . (*He looks at the ceiling*) And when you look up at the ceiling, it means, "What's the point of talking to her? She lives in her own world" . . . Perhaps that's because you think there's only *one* world. *Your* world . . . And because your world is very angry with me, I decided to stay in *my* world, hoping one day we could step out of *our* worlds and enter the *real* world . . . (*He turns, looks at her as if she didn't exist*) Don't look at me like that, Albert. I *hate* that look . . . If I called the police, they could arrest you for looking at me like that. (*He turns away*) I admit we did talk during the first *and* second marriage . . . Some . . . You were so hesitant about expressing yourself or revealing yourself . . . I know you got very angry when I suggested you find a doctor who specializes in "communicatively challenged" people . . . You were always sweet and gentle, Albert, but we had a vague marriage . . . It was like a window that needed washing. Something was out there but I could never see what . . . The only thing you were clear about was your silence and your silence was deafening . . . Why such a cruel punishment to me, Albert? Why? (*He goes to door, opens it, goes through and slams it. Then he reenters door and slams it. He repeats whole process and then he looks at her*) Because I walked out of the door twice, yes, I understand . . . But you know what I would have preferred, Albert? . . . That when you rang my doorbell, I would open it and you would call me the vilest names in the world . . . and then you would throw foul things at my feet . . . Things that even animals would walk around . . . and having said and done that, you'd be finished with me . . . and the past would be over with . . . is it possible for you to do that for me, Albert? Please? (*Albert looks at the floor*) All right, then don't speak to me. But do you have to seek me out and confront me everywhere? On the street, in shops, at the movies . . . If you'll release me from this torture, Albert, I'll give you anything you want . . . Not that I have much because I never took a penny from you for the divorce . . . Each divorce . . . But I'll beg, borrow or steal just to hear your voice again. (*She looks at him. He is still stony silent*) Say *something*, Albert. Move your lips, carve it in stone, drop leaflets from a plane, *write graffiti on my face with chalk*. But say *something*, damn it!! (*He suddenly holds up his index finger and writes a word in the air. She watches his finger*) You're spelling something . . . *Never*! . . . I see. (*He now spells the same word with the finger, more rapidly this time*) Never, never, never, never, yes I got it, Albert . . . Well, there's nothing left to say, is there? (*He points to himself, then points to the door*) You're leaving, yes, I understand . . . It was wonderful speaking to your finger, Albert.

(*Albert walks to the doorway, turns it halfway, then suddenly sneezes loudly*)

YVONNE (*without looking up*)**:** God bless you.

ALBERT (*as a reflex*)**:** Thank you. (*He leaves, closing the door behind him. Yvonne looks up, realizing what just happened. She stands*)

YVONNE: Was that him? Did he just say "Thank you?" . . . Oh, dear God. He spoke to me . . . *He spoke to me!!!*

(*The door reopens, Albert reenters, his head down in despair. He bangs on the door with his fist, angrily*)

ALBERT: I knew one day this would happen . . . But I *never* thought it would be like *this!*

(*He bangs door again*)

YVONNE: For whatever reason, even if you didn't mean it, it's over. Albert . . . You spoke to me.

ALBERT: I didn't *speak* to you. It was a reaction to God Bless You . . . If *you* had sneezed, I would have Gezuntheited you.

YVONNE: Still it's over, Albert. I'm free. I can breathe again.

ALBERT: You're *not* free. I was just being polite.

YVONNE: No, I'm free. Free free free. I'm free as a *bird.* (*She jumps and twirls through the air like a ballerina*) God bless you, Albert, my dear, sweet friend.

ALBERT: I spoke not because I wanted to. But because I couldn't take the pressure anymore.

YVONNE: Was your anger that great?

ALBERT: It was the only defense I had.

YVONNE: Defense against what?

ALBERT: Against admitting to myself that I still loved you. Still wanted you . . . If I kept silent, unapproachable, I would have built a wall so high, it would keep me safe from you forever.

YVONNE: What's safer than two divorces, Albert? . . . I'm sorry I caused you so much pain.

ALBERT: Not talking to you kept me from not wanting you.

YVONNE: Why do you still want me?

ALBERT: I will *always* want you . . . but now I can survive without you . . . It's safe for me to say your name now. (*Cheerfully*) Hello, Yvonne. What's new, Yvonne? How've you been, Yvonne?

YVONNE: Oh, so so. Not much new. Saw a wonderful movie last week.

ALBERT: I know. I waited for you to come out and not say a word to you.

YVONNE: Yes, I saw you.

ALBERT: Please don't smile.

YVONNE: I'm not laughing at you.

ALBERT: I know. But your smile weakens my resolve.

YVONNE: Sorry . . . So, are you seeing anyone? Special, I mean.

ALBERT: Actually, yes. Well, very, very briefly. I'm not sure it will work out.

YVONNE: Who is she?

ALBERT: Mariette.

YVONNE: I thought you just met her.

ALBERT: Yes. I said it was very, very brief . . . What about you? Are you seeing anyone?

YVONNE: Well, you would know. You've been four steps behind me the entire year.

ALBERT: Partly hounding you and partly to protect you from unsuitable men . . . like me.

YVONNE: You weren't the wrong man, Albert. We were the wrong *couple* . . . And now that we've settled things, you'll never ever confront me on the street corners and other places, will you?

ALBERT: No. Never. (*They shake on it. Albert doesn't flinch*) It doesn't hurt with you!

YVONNE: Thank you . . . So since you've promised not to hound me anymore, I promise not to marry you a third time.

ALBERT: A third time? I don't have a friend close enough to *come* to a third wedding.

YVONNE: Then let's be grateful for little things.

ALBERT: It's nice talking to you again . . . without rancor and anger about—well, what I've done to you this year.

YVONNE: But I understand why you did it. I'm sure

you thought I was very cruel to you. (*Albert shrugs*) But in marriage, people are always cruel to each other.

ALBERT: I loved you all the time.

YVONNE: You *thought* you did. But many's the time I saw that "God, I dislike you intensely" look.

ALBERT: I never disliked you intensely.

YVONNE: In-*tense*-ly. Sometimes you would glare at me and your eyes would grit their pupils.

ALBERT: You can't grit your pupils. You'd go blind.

YVONNE: And you would flare your nostrils. And bite your lower lip. And bang the side of your head with your knuckles. (*She does it to show him. She flares her nostrils, bites her lower lip, and bangs the side of her head with her knuckles*) . . . You looked like a small gorilla that hadn't been fed in the zoo.

ALBERT: I *never* did that. *Ever.*

YVONNE: I have pictures of it.

ALBERT: You went and got your camera while I was banging my head with my knuckles?

YVONNE: Yes. You were furious with me because I was angry with you. And do you know what you did to *make* me that angry?

ALBERT: No, but I'm sure you have a picture of it.

YVONNE: I'll tell you what you did . . . You loved me too much.

ALBERT: I *loved* you too much? . . . How is a thing like that possible?

YVONNE: Because it was all about *your* feelings, *your* emotions, *your* need to tell me how wonderfully happy you were. Gushing all that love and devotion for me with, "God, I'm so lucky to have you. How did a man like me wind up with someone as great as you?" . . . Never *once* thinking that I may be having a terrible day but *no*, you're too busy *fawning* all over me to ask how *I'm* feeling.

ALBERT (*glares at her*)**:** I'm not going to take a picture of what you just said, but I could do a quick oil painting of how neurotic and deranged you are.

YVONNE: *I'm* deranged? (*She laughs*) Was I the one following me all around the city, running into me face to face, for the satisfaction of not saying a word to me?

ALBERT: If I didn't seek you out, how would you know I wasn't speaking to you? I had to chase you all over the city to let you know I was ignoring you.

YVONNE: Yes. To punish me for leaving you. But it was you who divorced *me*. Remember?

ALBERT: Who else would I divorce? The maid? She had already quit. And she quit because she disliked you intensely.

YVONNE: Oh, yes. I can feel it coming on again. I can hear every single word you're never going to say to me.

ALBERT: No. Running after you is too exhausting. Instead I'll write to you. Blank page after blank page.

YVONNE: And I'll answer you. I'll write *blanker* pages and speak silent words. I don't care anymore. Divorce me again. Get an invisible lawyer and sue me in a non-existing court. I've beat you at your own game, Albert . . . Go! Leave! I'll even say goodbye for you. (*She pantomimes writing on a wall*) "Farewell and goodbye" . . . This is the last time I shall be speaking to you, Albert. (*Albert walks to the door, turns*)

ALBERT: I'm sorry this happened, Yvonne. (*She turns her back to him*) Will you be staying for dinner?

(*She drops her shoulders, walks hunched over, looks at the sky, stretches her arms out, et cetera. All the things he did in silence but in an exaggerated way*)

ALBERT: Aren't you going to run over there and slam the door twice?

YVONNE: I don't want to be cruel to you . . . again.

ALBERT: Thank you . . . Well, goodbye then . . . Yvonne. (*He crosses to the door and as he goes, she looks at him, not wanting him to go . . . In an effort to stop him she sneezes, then turns away*)

YVONNE: Gezuntheit. (*His eyes are fixed on her to answer. She covers her face with her hands, trying not to let him see she is crying, but she doesn't answer*)

ALBERT: You don't have to cry. I'll finish it . . . God bless you . . . Goodbye . . . (*He goes. She removes her hands. Mariette comes back in*)

MARIETTE: I know. Never never never never. I heard.

YVONNE: God, I hate marriage. The loving isn't worth the misery.

MARIETTE: The sex isn't worth all the bother.

YVONNE: Do you know of *anyone* who's happily married?

MARIETTE: Yes. Two pandas in the London Zoo.

YVONNE: I like you, Mariette.

MARIETTE: I like you too, Yvonne.

YVONNE: Too bad they didn't invite just six women. We could have gotten along so well.

(*The door opens and Gabrielle enters. She is elegant,*

striking looking, dressed smartly, and brimming with confidence. It's hard not to like her)

GABRIELLE: Last one here, I hope. If not, I'll make a re-entrance . . . Hello. Gabrielle Buonocelli.

YVONNE: You must be number six.

GABRIELLE: Am I? Did I win a door prize?

MARIETTE: The sixth guest, she means.

GABRIELLE: I *know* what she meant. And you're Mariette Levieux.

MARIETTE: Why, yes. Have we met?

GABRIELLE: No. We're meeting now. Are you related to *Charles* Levieux?

MARIETTE: He was my father.

GABRIELLE: Was?

MARIETTE: He died five years ago.

GABRIELLE: I'm sorry. I dated him when I was seventeen. I hope that doesn't offend you.

MARIETTE: No, but it might offend my mother.

GABRIELLE: I understand. I offended my mother, too . . . Your father was a true gentleman. Nothing happened. I can vouch for that. I even kept the voucher. (*To Yvonne*): And this pretty little thing must be Yvonne.

YVONNE: Yes. Yvonne Fouchet.

GABRIELLE: Was your father *Bernard* Fouchet?

YVONNE: No.

GABRIELLE: Good. Then we don't have to get into all that . . . And where are the three little mice?

MARIETTE: If you mean the men, they're sitting at the bar.

GABRIELLE: If they were men, they'd be sitting in here.

YVONNE: They wanted to leave, but we're all waiting for you.

GABRIELLE: Am I that important?

MARIETTE: You are if this dinner party was your idea.

YVONNE: Is it? I mean you *did* know Mariette's name and mine. And you asked where the men were and not *who* they were . . . You don't seem surprised by anything.

GABRIELLE (*She pours champagne for Mariette and Yvonne and hands it to them. She then pours her* *own*): There are no surprises in life. Just corroboration of what you suspected. Yes, I did know who was going to be here and why. As to who thought of this dinner party, I can tell you that as well . . . It was Andre Bouville's wife.

MARIETTE: His wife? He said she was dead.

GABRIELLE: Yes. It was a request from the grave. They were her last words.

YVONNE: She said, "Please, let's have a dinner party" and then died?

GABRIELLE: Well, perhaps not her *very* last words. She lingered on for another six months but didn't say anything worth quoting . . . I *do* know the actual invitations were sent by Paul Gerard.

MARIETTE: But why would she include us? We didn't know her.

GABRIELLE: The Greeks say the dead have their reasons.

(She pours herself some champagne as Mariette and Yvonne look at each other puzzled)

MARIETTE: If she couldn't come, why would she still have it?

GABRIELLE: They also say, even if you're dead, once you book it it's bad luck to cancel.

MARIETTE: If I'm not too impertinent, may I ask why *you're* here?

GABRIELLE: To look after the late Madame Bouville's interests.

(*She begins to cross to hors d'oeuvres*)

YVONNE: What interests? What could be left between Andre and his ex-dead wife?

GABRIELLE: His unfulfilled remorse.

YVONNE: But isn't it too late to give it to her now?

GABRIELLE: Yes, but it could be put into an account and given to some other deserving dead wife.

YVONNE (*aside to Mariette*)**:** She's strange, don't you think?

MARIETTE: Tell me about it.

YVONNE: Ask how she died.

GABRIELLE: You girls won't like hearing it.

YVONNE: I know. Tell it anyway.

GABRIELLE: Andre drove a stake through her heart . . . He was in a foul mood that day.

YVONNE: Are you saying he's a murderer?

GABRIELLE: Well, people who do business with him think he is. (*Looks at her watch*) Do you think we should call the boys in?

MARIETTE: I'm sorry, but has this murder been reported to anyone?

GABRIELLE: Yes, I just reported it to you . . .

YVONNE: I'm really having trouble with this . . . Why did he kill her?

GABRIELLE: Oh, she was unfaithful to him . . . And he couldn't forgive her.

YVONNE: It doesn't sound like he did.

GABRIELLE: On the other hand, he was unfaithful to her . . . but she *did* forgive him.

YVONNE: If you ask me, I think they deserved each other.

GABRIELLE: Don't judge them. Love is not an emotion shared only by the best people . . . The unscrupulous are as entitled to love as anyone else.

MARIETTE: You seem to have extraordinary sympathy for two people who were less than savory.

GABRIELLE: It's true they didn't have a shred of decency. But if you're a maggot, is it wrong to love another maggot?

YVONNE: Who was she?

GABRIELLE: A poor girl. As poor as he was once. They scraped the bottom of the same dirty barrel . . . What's the expression? Grime always rises to find its own level.

YVONNE: But I mean, *who* was she? What was her name?

GABRIELLE: She was born Constanza Buonocelli, but my friends call me Gabrielle.

YVONNE: Gabrielle? . . . You mean it's you?

GABRIELLE: Was I being obscure? Sorry. After twelve years of marriage, he suddenly left me for a more innocent version of me, fifteen years younger. I said I'd die before I gave him a divorce. As he left, he said, "Very well, Gabrielle, then I shall consider you dead" . . . If that doesn't feel like a stake through the heart, tell me what does.

YVONNE: And you still want him back?

GABRIELLE: Why not? I never stopped loving him. It was never his looks that attracted me. It was his mind. I find that brilliance and murkiness is an aphrodisiac.

MARIETTE: You can love a man who thinks of you as a corpse?

GABRIELLE: Why does love have to be so conventional? Wouldn't the world have cheered if the Elephant Man found an Elephant Woman?

MARIETTE: Is that how you see yourself? As the Elephant Woman?

GABRIELLE: God, no. I dress too well for that.

YVONNE: How did you two meet?

GABRIELLE: Gloriously! Like two bats crashing into each other in a cave.

MARIETTE: And do you actually expect that Andre will want you back?

GABRIELLE: I don't expect it. I predict it.

YVONNE: How can you be sure?

GABRIELLE: I can't. But my attitude is good.

MARIETTE: Then what took you so long in approaching him?

GABRIELLE: He'd never agree to meet me. And he's clever enough to escape any chance meeting I planned. But he'll play this out tonight because of his respect for Paul Gerard.

YVONNE: But where's the romance in all this? He seems so cold and callous. Don't you yearn for tenderness?

GABRIELLE: We're not tender people. Once, in the heat of passion, I had my big toe broken. I don't know how it happened but for years we tried to repeat it.

MARIETTE: Are you saying you're a masochist?

GABRIELLE: Not at all. I don't enjoy pain. I just like the pursuit of it. Well, I think it's time Andre and I met.

(*Yvonne looks at Mariette, hoping somehow to understand all this*)

YVONNE: Shall I tell him you're here?

GABRIELLE: He knows.

YVONNE: He saw you?

GABRIELLE: He senses me. We can sense each other a mile away. Saves us a fortune on phone calls.

(*The door opens. Claude comes in*)

CLAUDE: Excuse me, but I have a message from Andre. (*He sees Gabrielle*) Oh. Hello. I'm Claude Pichon.

GABRIELLE: And I'm Gabrielle, the late Madame Bouville.

CLAUDE: Oh, you're not that late. Five minutes or so.

MARIETTE (*to Claude*)**:** As you can see, Claude, she's not deceased.

CLAUDE: Yes. You writers are so observant. (*To Gabrielle*) Does it bother you that Andre told us you were dead?

GABRIELLE: Oh, no. We always called each other pet names . . . I can see you've spotted his flaws, haven't you?

CLAUDE: His mouth leaves tracks wherever he goes . . . Well, whatever world you're in, he'd like a word with you in private.

YVONNE (*to Claude*)**:** Does Albert still think she's dead? He'll walk in here thinking it's a séance.

MARIETTE (*to Yvonne*)**:** That's very good, Yvonne.

YVONNE: Thank you. I'm rarely ever funny.

GABRIELLE (*to Claude*)**:** Please tell my ex-husband I'm very anxious to have him join me . . . from whence he sent me.

CLAUDE (*to Gabrielle*)**:** I think it fair to tell you that it's Albert's and my opinion that as soon as you two have your talk, this dinner party is over.

GABRIELLE: I think not. The six of us made a promise to Paul Gerard to see this thing through.

CLAUDE: Since this is now a confrontation between

you and Andre, it doesn't really concern us. And I'll be glad to tell that to Andre. (*To Mariette*) If I don't see you again, Mariette, I thought I'd just say—that I probably won't see you again. (*He goes, closing door*)

MARIETTE: He is *so* dreary.

GABRIELLE: Don't be too hard on him. He must have picked it up from Andre.

YVONNE: I wish I were more like you, Gabrielle.

GABRIELLE: No, you don't dear. We need people like you to balance out people like me.

YVONNE: Meaning I'm boring? Is that meant as an insult?

GABRIELLE: Yes, but in a positive way. A woman who isn't insulted now and then ceases to be interesting.

(*The door opens and a hostile Andre comes in, staring at Gabrielle*)

GABRIELLE: Oh, hello, Andre. I'm sorry. I really tried staying dead for you but the spirit wasn't willing . . . Angry?

ANDRE: Not even surprised. I saw your hand in this from the beginning. (*To Mariette and Yvonne*) Can you ladies hear all this or shall I speak louder?

YVONNE: No, I can hear you fine.

MARIETTE: Which is why we're leaving. (*To Gabrielle*) Gabrielle, I just wanted to say, don't let anyone—

GABRIELLE: I know. And I thank you for not saying it.

YVONNE (*to Mariette*)**:** Not saying what? (*The two ladies leave, closing the side door behind them*)

GABRIELLE (*to Andre*)**:** No compliments, Andre? Considering I had to push aside a heavy gravestone, don't you think I look stunning?

ANDRE: When was stunning ever your problem? . . . and not even a twenty-foot marble mausoleum could stop you . . . Alright, you have your life back again. In exchange, may I please have the freedom the courts have already awarded me?

GABRIELLE: Just because they're overgenerous doesn't mean *I* have to be.

ANDRE: It's been two years. The relationship is long over Gabrielle. Put it to bed, will you?

GABRIELLE: You first. I always liked crawling in after you warmed up the sheets.

ANDRE: Can't you take a simple divorce as a "no"?

GABRIELLE: I'm not happy with the settlement.

ANDRE: You have half the company, what more do you want?

GABRIELLE: Keep the company. It's the boss I want . . . and the rest of our lives together that you promised me. You've had your vacation, Andre. Mommy wants you back home.

ANDRE: My "mommy's" in Switzerland and delighted not to receive those vulgar Christmas presents from you anymore.

GABRIELLE: Your mother hasn't the slightest idea of what a monster she gave birth to. And my mother died before she knew I was in love with one. Isn't it sweet to know we were so good to our mothers?

ANDRE: Do you really enjoy hounding me?

GABRIELLE: We've done doggy things before, you never complained.

ANDRE: I know this won't ruffle you a bit, but you do disgust me sometimes.

GABRIELLE: Why not now? You always preferred your pleasure in the most unlikely places.

ANDRE: Call this night off. These people don't want to be with each other. Nothing will come of it. It's graceless and self-serving on your part.

GABRIELLE: Self-serving is what kept you and me

alive. I want this dinner party. Let's wait and see till we've all been put to the test.

ANDRE: Oh? Are you going to spring something dreadful on us? Leaving shattered lives all over La Cassette's dining room floor? My God, Gabrielle, you've become a caricature of yourself and it makes me sad.

GABRIELLE: You sad? Then this has to be a first for you. I've never seen a teardrop made of ice.

ANDRE: When did I ever claim to be boyish and unassuming? We were what we were. Two termites eating away at each others' innards until our structure collapsed. No. I never want to set foot in that condemned house again.

GABRIELLE: Honey, you don't even have to ring the bell. I could have you back in a second, but I'd rather toy with you first.

ANDRE (*amused*)**:** Do you really think you're that clever?

GABRIELLE: I'm not clever at all. I'm just that determined.

ANDRE: Oh, stop it, Gabrielle. I feel like I'm talking to a machine that spits out poisoned tennis balls.

GABRIELLE: Why do you keep playing the role of the innocent bystander? You've left your fingerprints on every deliciously sordid pleasure we indulged in.

ANDRE: Which you seemed to want desperately. Whatever we did, we did with mutual consent. You never knew when to stop.

GABRIELLE: No, but when I did, you were always ever ready to replace the batteries.

ANDRE: Oh, for Chris' sake, can't you say a simple declarative sentence without squeezing it out of your brain like some demented toothpaste.

GABRIELLE: Demented? Yes, I suppose I was at times. Sickening, isn't it, what some women will do for good company.

ANDRE: Just tell me, what kind of hopeless gesture do you want out of this party? And why did you drag these puzzled minor players into your plot? Are they to be witnesses to your day of revenge, fulfulled or not?

GABRIELLE: Sometimes, when I look at you, I wonder, is your spark diminishing, or are you getting older?

ANDRE: Getting older, I think. Would it surprise you to hear that I *like* getting older? I don't want to work that hard anymore. I don't want to *live* that hard . . . and I certainly don't want to *play* that hard.

GABRIELLE: Neither do I. My waist can't keep pretending to fit the dresses you so ardently and rapaciously unzipped for me . . . So what is it you *do* want?

ANDRE: I want a wife. A *wifely* wife . . . Someone who'll let me sleep through the night. Someone who'll think staying home means a good time to read or having a conversation that doesn't require heavy breathing . . . And someone who'll give me what I suddenly and surprisingly yearn for . . . Children.

GABRIELLE (*hurt by this*)**:** I was *never* against having children.

ANDRE: With us as parents? They'd wake up Christmas morning playing with tarantulas.

GABRIELLE: I've satisfied your every whim for twelve years and suddenly you've grown tired of whimsy . . . I was tired of it *years* ago, but I never complained for fear of losing you . . . I never minded being your favorite horse in the stable, Andre, but I'll be damned if I'll let you go to pasture without me.

ANDRE: I'm getting married next month.

GABRIELLE: I can stand a minor interruption.

ANDRE: I'm serious about this woman.

GABRIELLE: She'll get over it . . . I've half seduced you already. A month ago you wouldn't have taken my phone call. Yet now, you're standing in front of me, glued to the floor.

ANDRE: Just to tell you that for the first time, I know what real love is.

GABRIELLE: Love is easy, Andre. Eternal desire, however, is a bitch to break.

ANDRE (*starts to walk out, then turns, deciding to confront her*)**:** Our desire, as you call it, turned ugly somewhere along the line, and we both suffered for it . . . I stopped making love *with* you, but rather *at* you . . . I used your body as an outlet for all my repressed anger. Your womb became a receptacle of all my self-loathing for not being able to break the hold you had on me . . . I *plunged* everything into you like an animal, not to possess you, but to use force against you so that you'd have no other choice but to let me loose . . . And in trying to assuage my guilt, I made you my partner in crime . . . Let go of me, Gabrielle, and you'll win your self-respect back . . . Let go of me, and you'll be able to return to that fork in the road, where we once, many years ago, went wrong.

GABRIELLE (*moving very close to him*)**:** If I have that much power, do you know what that makes me, Andre? A witch . . . and only the Son of Satan can make a witch. (*He suddenly grabs her and kisses her, pressing against her lips . . . then pushes her away, knowing she still holds a power over him*) Sorry, Andre. The dinner party goes on. (*She crosses to the dining table, moving tantalizingly around the table,* *touching each chair as if she were taunting Andre)* Divorcee, ex-husband, divorcee, ex-husband, divorcee, ex-husband . . .

(*The door opens and Claude and Albert come in*)

CLAUDE: Well, we're splitting—which is what we all did in the first place.

GABRIELLE (*to Albert*)**:** Albert Donay, am I right? Oh, what a pity, Albert. Mariette was hoping she'd sit next to you.

ALBERT: She said that?

GABRIELLE: At least twice. I've got you and Mariette seated over there so you can avoid not talking to Yvonne . . . Claude, please stay and sit on my right. I'm *really* anxious to get to know you better.

CLAUDE (*to Andre*)**:** Any thoughts on that, Andre?

ANDRE: Do it. I think someone like you deserves someone like her.

(*The side door opens and Mariette and Yvonne enter*)

CLAUDE (*sees them*)**:** Ah! Act Three. The mystery unravels.

MARIETTE: It unraveled two years ago, honey.

YVONNE: So do we sit anywhere or is it pot luck?

GABRIELLE: No. Don't sit yet. I'm still rearranging . . . Just move around, let me think this out.

CLAUDE: Move around?

GABRIELLE: Please. (*They indulge her. Confused and annoyed, they look at each other as they circle about, not wishing to make contact . . . Gabrielle watches . . . and then shouts*) *Stop!!* (*They all stop*) Now this is interesting. Notice how we've all lined up. (*They all look at each other*) For some reason, we're all facing each other's former spouse. (*They have*) Now why do you think that is?

CLAUDE: You put magnets under the floor.

ALBERT: I guess I should be facing Yvonne *twice.*

ANDRE: And what do we do now? The Divorced Couples Polka?

YVONNE: No. It's women facing men. Against each other. It's been that way since Adam and Eve.

CLAUDE: Adam and Eve never got divorced. They were forced to move because of that apple trouble.

GABRIELLE: Can I try something? Sort of a game.

CLAUDE: If I'm not staying for dinner, why would I stay for a game?

GABRIELLE: Because it's a dangerous game. Do

you like danger, Claude? Of course you do. Sit, stand, whatever you want. Make yourselves comfortable. (*They look at each other again, then move. Some sit, some stand. Andre leans against the wall. Albert sits at the dining table. Gabrielle stands, running the show*) Thank you . . . now here's the game . . . What if this were the first time we all met? Would we all have chosen the same one we had before?

(*Claude laughs sardonically. Andre shakes his head futilely*)

CLAUDE: No. I would have picked Andre. At least I'd get most of my alimony back.

ALBERT: I wouldn't have picked anyone. If I had to do it over, I'd become a monk.

YVONNE: That's because they don't speak to anyone either.

MARIETTE: Well, I wouldn't pick Claude because nothing would change. And if I *did* pick him, I'd end up at a party like this explaining why I wouldn't pick him.

ANDRE: Did you know that primates are more successful at choosing their mates than we are? And rarely separate.

CLAUDE: That's because there're not as many lawyers in the jungle.

GABRIELLE: But we *did* marry. We *did* make the choice. I'm just curious as to why we all went wrong?

ALBERT: I don't know. Would anyone mind if I took my dinner home? I'll eat it later.

ANDRE: Good idea. Let's share a cab. (*Andre crosses to the front door, tries the knob. It doesn't open*)

GABRIELLE: It's locked, darling. From the outside. My orders once we were all in here. Cost me a pretty penny but I will have my dinner party.

ANDRE (*has crossed to side door. Tries knob*)**:** This one's locked as well.

GABRIELLE: In for a penny, in for a pound.

CLAUDE (*picks up the restaurant phone*)**:** She must be dotty. Hello? . . . Hello? . . . This line is out.

GABRIELLE: That one was complimentary. They like me here.

CLAUDE: We're locked in? It's a goddamn Agatha Christie dinner.

MARIETTE: Listen, I have a phobia about closed doors . . . Seriously.

GABRIELLE: Well, if we're all ready, shall we begin?

ALBERT: Begin what?

GABRIELLE: The investigation of whether we think our divorces were a mistake or not.

CLAUDE: Big. Big mistake. Trust me. Just take a group picture of us all.

GABRIELLE: But let's say one couple, just one, decides to go back together again . . . or even makes the effort to *try* it once more . . . How insane would that be?

CLAUDE: What's the highest number you'd accept?

ALBERT: I tried it twice. The wedding rings are costing me a fortune.

GABRIELLE: Mariette? I'd love to hear your opinion.

MARIETTE: I don't have an opinion, I have claustrophobia. I can't think until you open the door or the windows.

ANDRE: There *are* no windows. Just air vents.

(*Mariette starts reaching up for the air vent*)

GABRIELLE: Yvonne?

YVONNE: I might reconsider marrying. But not Albert. Maybe Andre, or Claude, or one of the waiters, but definitely not Albert.

CLAUDE: Why not a vote? A show of hands to decide who wants to do this.

GABRIELLE: Fair enough. All those who would consider the possibility of a trial reunion with their spouse, raise your hand. (*No one does except Gabrielle. Her hand goes straight up. Mariette's is up because she's reaching for the air vent. Gabrielle looks around*) Well, we have two hands. This shows that not everyone is against this.

CLAUDE (*aside to Andre*)**:** Now I can understand why you're so ill-tempered.

GABRIELLE: I have a rather interesting question to ask everyone. An early response could lead to an early settlement. May I?

ALBERT: This isn't about us. It's about you and Andre . . . Why don't we lock you two up and we'll all go home.

GABRIELLE: I think it's about *all* of us. A few minutes, that's all I'm asking.

YVONNE: What's your question?

GABRIELLE: But you'll all have to be ruthlessly honest.

MARIETTE: *Ask it! Ask it!* I'm beginning to circulate my own breath. *Ask it!*

GABRIELLE: I would like to ask each one of us here, to tell us the worst thing your ex-spouse ever did to you during your marriage.

(*They all look at each other*)

CLAUDE (*throws up his hands*)**:** Well, we can all kiss *this* night goodbye.

GABRIELLE: Remember! The worst thing your ex-spouse ever did to you.

ALBERT: At a dinner party? It's too personal. Maybe we should all go to a church and squeeze into a confessional box.

GABRIELLE: Any volunteers? (*There are none*) Well, I don't mind being the first . . . Alright, I'd like to tell you the worst thing that Andre ever did to me during our marriage.

ANDRE: Careful, Gabrielle.

GABRIELLE (*to Andre*)**:** Oh? Afraid I'm going to vilify you, Andre? (*To others*) Am I going too far? Would you rather not hear what Andre did to me?

(*Of course they want to hear*)

CLAUDE: Well, we're all locked in, we're not going anywhere. Might as well tell us. (*He sits*)

GABRIELLE: Now then . . . The worst thing that Andre ever did to me during our marriage . . . was to make me love him unconditionally. (*They all look a little disappointed*)

ALBERT: That's it? . . . We got locked up to hear *that*?

CLAUDE: My *dog* loves me unconditionally. But she wouldn't lock us up in a restaurant.

YVONNE: Let her finish.

GABRIELLE: We lived our lives on the brink of destruction. We each agreed that no matter what, we'd see it through. And to survive, you had to commit yourself completely. Body and soul . . . To trust each other, our love had to be unquestioned. We were prisoners for life, each to the other . . . I willingly complied. Andre made a sacred vow . . . And one day, he lost his nerve . . . And when he left me, he robbed me of the ability to hate him . . . or to be happy without him . . . I'm stuck with loving him and that's a vicious thing to do to anyone.

(*They are all silent for a moment*)

YVONNE: . . . I really didn't think we were going to get *that* personal.

ANDRE: You're as free as I am. Love is a state of mind, not a legal agreement . . . Neither of us was bound together for life . . . She's free to stop loving me anytime she wants. She has a fixation that can be treated by a good analyst, a guru, an exorcist, or a new hair stylist.

(*He turns, walks away. Albert raises his hand*)

ALBERT (*to Gabrielle*)**:** Excuse me, but is this how you thought you'd get couples back together again?

GABRIELLE: I told the truth. Andre's truth, like his menswear, fits his style.

MARIETTE: Do what you want. I'm ready to get on my knees and suck air from under the door.

CLAUDE: Okay . . . I'll play . . . Would you all like to hear the worst thing Mariette did to me in our marriage?

MARIETTE: Just don't use up too much oxygen.

CLAUDE: I'll be quick. It's just one sentence . . . At a book party in her honor, Mariette was about to introduce me to her publisher . . . and forgot my name.

MARIETTE: I said Claude.

CLAUDE: No, *I* said Claude. You looked at me blankly and your eyes said, "Help me, whoever you are."

MARIETTE: It was my first book party, for God's sake. I was petrified. I didn't purposely do it.

CLAUDE: No. But I think your subconscious said, "I wish you weren't here."

MARIETTE: No. My subconscious said, "I wish you *were* here and proud of me." But I knew you were thinking, "Why is this cheap publishing house publishing her cheap novel."

CLAUDE: That was *your* thought, not mine. Interesting how thoughts are more honest than words.

MARIETTE: In your heart, you wanted me to fail as a writer, something you were too frightened to do on your own. So you denied me your support and affection . . . No, the worst thing I ever did to Claude, was to fulfill my own dream.

CLAUDE: Not quite true, but thanks for remembering my name.

MARIETTE (*angrily*)**:** I didn't remember it. I just took a wild guess.

YVONNE: . . . The worst thing Albert ever did? . . . One night we had a terrible fight. Albert found some love letters I hid in my closet . . . He read them all. In his anger, he threw them into the fireplace and set them ablaze. They were all destroyed . . . My dearest and most cherished possessions and I've lost them forever.

GABRIELLE: May I ask who the letters were from?

YVONNE: From Albert. Who else would they *be* from? . . . He never explained why. In the morning I burned all his ties. I didn't explain why either.

(*They all look puzzled*)

MARIETTE: My turn. How's this? Claude had an affair with my sister . . . Great beginning, don't you think?

CLAUDE: Mariette . . . there's no need to go into that.

MARIETTE: We've heard yours, honeybunch, why not mine? . . . It went on for over a year. Claude and my sister Germaine . . . At least he didn't go outside the family.

YVONNE: I don't exactly consider that a plus.

ALBERT: And this affair . . . Did you let it continue?

MARIETTE: I was hurt, of course, but when I saw it was what he needed, I let it continue.

ALBERT: Where did they go? To her place? Did you follow them? She was attractive, I suppose.

CLAUDE: Oh. Finally a subject he wants to paint.

MARIETTE: I let them use our house. Our bedroom.

ANDRE: Do you enjoy hearing this, Gabrielle?

MARIETTE: No. Actually *I* do. I've been wanting to tell someone for years.

ALBERT (*to Mariette*)**:** And while they were—you know—where did you go?

MARIETTE: I stayed in the room, of course. It couldn't happen without my being there.

ANDRE: Are you saying you watched?

MARIETTE: No. I participated. I have no sister. But Claude invented one, which was the only fiction he ever came up with.

CLAUDE: Christ.

MARIETTE: So I became Germaine, the name he gave her. I preferred Rene, but it was his fantasy.

CLAUDE: What man doesn't have a fantasy? What woman for that matter?

GABRIELLE (*to Mariette*)**:** Having a fantasy with your own wife isn't exactly infidelity. Surely everyone in this room must have had one.

ALBERT: I've only had one. This is it. Hearing something like this from a woman. Wow.

CLAUDE: Wow? Did he say *wow*? How did he get in here?

MARIETTE: I had my own fantasy. That I would be enough for Claude. But a long marriage eventually takes its toll, so I played Germaine for him. It got out of hand. He bought me a bathrobe with her name on it. Negligees with her initials. He was more passionate, infinitely freer with her than he ever was with me. I saw an analyst to find out what Germaine was giving him that I couldn't . . . And soon I despised Mariette because she was too weak to fight her rival . . . His jealousy of my success. The lack of his own and his unwillingness to give up

Germaine, finally led to our divorce . . . So that's my little story . . . What a swell party this is.

(*It is silent for a moment. Then Albert looks at Claude*)

ALBERT (*raises his hand*)**:** . . . So Claude, do you still see Germaine?

CLAUDE: No, but I could introduce you, you horny little bastard.

ANDRE: All right, boys. Let's either grow up or shut up.

GABRIELLE: And as for you, Andre, it's time for you to *own* up . . . What was the worst thing I ever did to you?

(*He takes his time* . . .)

ANDRE: . . . That you let us continue. That you never asked *me* for a divorce. That you let me degrade you in the name of love . . . or lust . . . There was nothing too vile for you to indulge in to satisfy my voracious appetite . . . You let me use you at the cost of your own dignity and self-esteem . . . You can't imagine the loathing I felt for myself . . . That's the worst thing you ever did to me . . . and the fact that I'm able to reveal this to total strangers, is proof that my malady lingers on. (*He looks at her*) Satisfied, Gabrielle? So tell us. Who won?

GABRIELLE: No one won. We all lost. Every one of us.

MARIETTE: It's over. Thank God. Open the doors. I was ready to start breathing through my ears.

ALBERT: Excuse me. You forgot me. About the worst thing Yvonne ever did to me?

GABRIELLE: You're right. I'm sorry. Tell us, Albert.

ALBERT (*to Gabrielle*)**:** How is it possible you left me out?

CLAUDE: We took a secret ballot . . . Just tell it, will you?

ALBERT (*to Claude*)**:** Andre was right about you from the beginning. (*To everyone*). . . I burned my letters, because I thought Yvonne deserved better. I wanted her to have poetry that could capture everything that was exquisite about her . . . As I matured, I began to write new ones. This time I found my voice. This time I wrote—with passion, with love and clarity . . . They came from the deepest part of my soul . . . And on the envelopes, I drew wonderful sketches of her face . . . without a used car in sight . . . When I had enough letters, I put them on her bedstand, to read when she awoke.

GABRIELLE: And did she?

ALBERT: It made no difference. I found a letter from her on *my* bedstand . . . asking for a divorce . . . I never got a chance to explain why I burned my letters . . . But I guess it was all over on the morning she burned all my ties . . . That was the worst thing she ever did to me . . . Since then I've moved on with my life.

MARIETTE: Are we through?

GABRIELLE: We're not quite finished. There's still one more question to be asked . . .

CLAUDE: Oh, God. It's like a self-help group. You pay five hundred dollars for the weekend and they don't let you pee until Monday morning.

YVONNE: What's the question, Gabrielle? Tell us what the question is . . . Please, for God's sake. *Ask the fucking question* . . . If I just said what I think I did, please forgive me.

GABRIELLE: The question is simply this . . . What is the *nicest* thing your spouse ever did for you during your marriage? . . . Any volunteers? . . . Has no one here done a decent thing for their spouse? Ever? (*No answer*). . . Then I've been wrong. (*She crosses to the door*) Sorry I've wasted your evening. (*She unlocks the door*) It's open. Freedom is just outside.

(*Claude and Andre look at each other, then start for the door*)

YVONNE: Well . . . There *was* something Albert used to do.

GABRIELLE (*to Claude and Andre*)**:** Wait! Please.

Just hear Yvonne out. (*Reluctantly they stop, hover near door*) Yvonne.

YVONNE: He would bring me a warm croissant and hot tea every morning. Then he would sit on the bed and look at me. Lovingly. His eyes were warmer than the croissant . . . and his hands touching mine were more soothing than the honey he stirred in my tea . . . No matter what cruel things I may have said to him the day before, I knew I would wake in the morning and find breakfast and Albert in front of me on the bed . . . and I felt more love than I ever thought was possible . . . Even on the morning when I left the note saying I was leaving, he still brought me my morning breakfast . . . He didn't say a word but I could see the tears in his eyes as I left . . . I will always remember you for that, Albert . . . Always.

CLAUDE: We all will, Al . . . Gabrielle? No more parties, okay?

(*He starts to go*)

MARIETTE: *Sit down, Claude!!* Or I'll tell them about my twin sisters, Lily and Milly. (*Embarrassed, he sits down. As does Andre*) . . . On our third anniversary, Claude took me to the restaurant where we first met. (*Claude looks up at Mariette*) He gave me a pair of exquisite earrings from Cartier . . . but as beautiful as they were, it was his note that touched me . . . I remember every word . . . "To My Dearest Mariette . . . If I were never born, I would have still found a way to love you . . . If we never met, I would have kept on looking, *hoping* to find you . . . If I died, I would sit on some distant cloud, ignoring my heavenly duties, to watch over you . . . and if I lost you, through my own foolishness, I would forfeit my eternal peace, to win your forgiveness . . . Your devoted and loving husband, Claude" (*She touches her ears*) Interesting that I should be wearing those same earrings tonight, isn't it?

(*Another moment of silence*)

ALBERT: I—I want to do this . . . I'm just not ready yet . . . Someone else . . . please.

CLAUDE (*clears his throat*)**:** I was more confident in my prose in those days . . . but I think that the most endearing thing that my ex—that Mariette ever did for me, was not during our marriage, but for what she did just now . . . for remembering the best of me, instead of all my accusations against her before . . . She is a graceful woman, even under fire . . . and in case she's still interested, I realized soon after our divorce, that it was not Germaine that I wanted at all.

(*He wants to say more but doesn't. He walks away*)

GABRIELLE: Albert? Andre? Anything to say . . . Not yet? . . . In that case, let me tell you the nicest thing Andre ever did for me in our marriage . . . I can say it in one word . . . Everything! . . . It may not be everything that someone *else* would want, but it depends on how you choose to perceive it . . . He wouldn't stand up to the scrutiny under a microscope, so I avoided the microscope and accepted him just as he was . . . As I said, I loved him unconditionally because conditionally would have destroyed us . . . I loved him not *despite* his shortcomings, but because he never tried to conceal them . . . I knew what I was getting and what I got was what I wanted . . . I never separated the good days with him from the bad days, as long as I had *all* the days with him. He's not a kind man but he's the kind of man who suits the kind of woman I am . . . I pray to Almighty God, who I don't think approved of us very much, to let me have the *rest* of my days with him. His gift to me was to make me feel alive and for what I got, Andre, I thank you . . . For what I'll *get*—well, we'll just have to wait, won't we?

(*She crosses to a safe spot, not wanting to be in the spotlight just now. They look at Albert*)

ALBERT: I'm still working on mine. Andre, you can have the floor.

ANDRE: . . . I think this night has been an aberration. An embarrassment to human behavior . . . Nevertheless, I contributed to it, so yes, I will have my say about Gabrielle . . . Tonight was all her idea, her brainchild, her impossible dream . . . and for some reason, I think some good will come of it . . . Some of us will take a second look at ourselves, of what we had and what we lost . . . and some may make a decision which would have seemed inconceivable before we arrived here tonight . . . What's the nicest thing Gabrielle did for me? . . . That I could commit no sin against her, as long as I was honest. I know what and who I am only because she made me look at myself without dodging the truth . . . Her perspective on what is truthful is infallible . . . For what it's worth, Gabrielle, you deserve more kindness than you've ever received . . .

(*They catch each other's gaze, then he looks away*)

ALBERT: . . . So, it comes down to me, right? . . . Okay. About Yvonne. . . She told me earlier tonight that when we were married, I loved her too much . . . So? Shouldn't I be the judge of how much to love someone? . . . It's my heartache, I'll deal with it . . . But what I *didn't* see, was that if she loved me 100 percent, and I loved her one hundred and *forty* percent, she could never catch up to me . . . I realize now that bringing someone a warm croissant and hot tea *every single morning* . . . was *more* than loving . . . it was *stifling* . . . Maybe she wanted eggs one morning . . . or toast and jam . . . or maybe nothing . . . and I wouldn't let her have nothing . . . but she was too loving a wife to deny me my pleasure . . . And maybe that's why she left me . . . And when she came back the second time, instead, I brought her hot biscuits and cocoa . . . every *single* morning. So I think the nicest thing she ever did for me, was to leave me the second time . . . because it finally got through to me . . . to let her make her own choices . . . Well, I didn't get a third chance, and I know I never will . . . because after a year of not talking to her, now I don't seem to be able to stop . . . But I will . . . Thank you for listening, Yvonne.

CLAUDE: Is that it? Are we through?

GABRIELLE: We're through . . . Thank you all for indulging me . . . I'm staying for dinner . . . If any . . . or all of you want to join me, I'd be delighted . . . Please allow me the pleasure of seating you, if you're staying . . . (*She crosses behind chair at the head of the table*) I'll sit here at the head . . . Mariette? Would—would you care to sit here?

(*They all look at Mariette. She seems undecided, then*)

MARIETTE: Yes. Thank you, Gabrielle. (*She crosses to her seat*)

GABRIELLE: Albert? Here, if you don't mind.

(*He looks at Yvonne, then at Gabrielle*)

ALBERT: I don't mind at all. (*He crosses to his seat*)

GABRIELLE: Claude?

CLAUDE: Er . . . Give me a moment to think, will you? Ask someone else.

GABRIELLE: Yvonne? Over here opposite Mariette?

YVONNE (*she looks at table, takes a step forward, then stops*)**:** I would like very much to . . . but I don't think I can go through all that again . . . Please forgive me. Goodnight, Gabrielle.

(*Hurriedly, she goes out the door. Albert is disappointed*)

GABRIELLE: Andre? . . . I thought here on my right . . . or wherever you'd like.

ANDRE: Yes. On your right would be fine . . . That is, if I were to stay . . . but I think we both know it's too late . . . I'm so sorry. (*He goes, closing the door behind him*)

GABRIELLE: Well . . . small parties can be fun too . . . Claude, have you made up your mind?

CLAUDE: Maybe I'll stay just for a bite . . . if that's all right with you, Mariette?

MARIETTE: Yes, it is all right with Mariette.

CLAUDE: Thank you. (*He crosses to his seat*)

GABRIELLE: Well, I do have *one* happy surprise. (*She picks up the restaurant phone and hears that it's working again*) At least we won't have to serve ourselves. (*Into phone*) Yes. It's Madame Buonocelli . . . You may send the waiters in, please . . . No . . . Just for four of us, it seems. (*She hangs up the phone. To others*) Well, not too bad. On a scale of six, we've still got sixty percent.

(*The door opens and Yvonne comes in, scurries to her chair across from Albert*)

YVONNE (*sits*)**:** Sorry. I would have changed my mind in the taxi anyway. (*To Albert*) If you don't mind, Albert, I'll order for myself.

(*Albert gives her a small smile. Gabrielle gets up, crossing to the closed door*)

GABRIELLE: I know you don't like being closed in, Mariette. Why don't I leave this door open . . . just in case. (*She opens the door, looks out, then crosses back to her seat. Sits, takes her napkin*) Well, now that we've gotten our business out of the way, maybe we can all get to know each other better. (*She smiles. Dim out*)

(*Curtain.*)